WALT DISNEY

By Joan Stoltman

Gareth Stevens
PUBLISHING

Please visit our website, www.garethstevens.com. For a free color catalog of all our high-quality books, call toll free 1-800-542-2595 or fax 1-877-542-2596.

Library of Congress Cataloging-in-Publication Data

Names: Stoltman, Joan, author.
Title: Walt Disney / Joan Stoltman.
Description: New York : Gareth Stevens Publishing, 2018. | Series: Little
  biographies of big people | Includes bibliographical references and index.
Identifiers: LCCN 2017025325| ISBN 9781538212431 (pbk.) | ISBN 9781538212448 (6 pack) |
ISBN 9781538212455 (library bound)
Subjects: LCSH: Disney, Walt, 1901-1966–Juvenile literature. |
  Animators–United States–Biography–Juvenile literature. | Animated
  films–United States–Juvenile literature.
Classification: LCC NC1766.U52 D5654 2018 | DDC 741.58092 [B] –dc23
LC record available at https://lccn.loc.gov/2017025325

Published in 2018 by
Gareth Stevens Publishing
111 East 14th Street, Suite 349
New York, NY 10003

Designer: Samantha DeMartin
Editor: Joan Stoltman

Photo credits: series art Yulia Glam/Shutterstock.com; cover, p. 1 GAB Archive/Redferns/
Getty Images; p. 5 Apic/Hulton Archive/Getty Images; pp. 7, 17 ullstein bild/ullstein bild/Getty
Images; pp. 9, 15 Hulton Archive/Archive Photos/Getty Images; p. 11 Michael Orso/Moment/
Getty Images; p. 13 (inset) Peter Stackpole/The LIFE Picture Collection/Getty Images;
p. 13 (main) Earl Theisen Collection/Archive Photos/Getty Images; p. 19 Bettmann/Bettmann/
Getty Images; p. 21 (North America) © traveler1116/iStockphoto.com; p. 21 (Europe)
Stamptastic/Shutterstock.com; p. 21 (Africa) rook76/Shutterstock.com; p. 21 (Asia) neftali/
Shutterstock.com.

Printed in the United States of America

CPSIA compliance information: Batch #CW18GS: For further information contact Gareth Stevens, New York, New York at 1-800-542-2595.

CONTENTS

Boldface words appear in the glossary.

Way Before Mickey

Walter Elias Disney was born in 1901 in Chicago, Illinois. He had three brothers and a sister. His family moved a lot because his dad changed jobs often. At one point, he lived on a farm. Walt loved the farm animals and his small town!

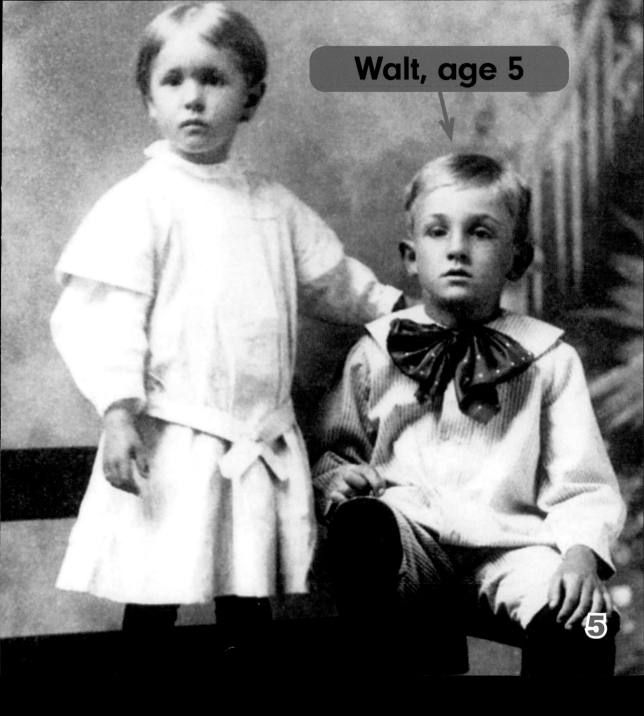

Walt loved to draw and paint! He sold his art to neighbors and traded it for haircuts. As a young teenager, he took art classes at the Kansas City Art **Institute**. During high school, Walt took night classes at the Art Institute of Chicago.

7

Walt Won't Quit

Walt's first adult job was drawing cartoons for **commercials**. He learned how to **animate**—and invented new ways to animate! Walt quit commercials and started his own animation company, Laugh-O-Grams. The company had **setbacks** and had to close. But that didn't stop Walt!

Finally, Success!

In 1923, Walt moved to Hollywood, California, with $40 in his pocket. He and his brother Roy started Disney Brothers' Cartoon Studio. They had several early setbacks. Then, in 1928, Walt created Mickey Mouse. Mickey was the first talking cartoon character ever!

"Partners"

"We believe in our idea: a family park where parents and children could have fun - together."

Walt Disney

11

Throughout the **Great Depression**, Walt's cartoons brought millions of people much-needed happiness. Next, he decided to make the first-ever full-length animated movie, *Snow White and the Seven Dwarfs*. Walt took a big chance, spending $1.5 million and 3 years on the movie.

13

When *Snow White* came out in 1937, it made $6.7 million and won many **awards**. Walt had turned animation into a new art form. Walt and Roy soon had over 1,000 people working for them so they could make more full-length movies!

Creating an Empire

Next, Walt had his studio make live-action color movies and TV. His love of animals led him to direct one of the first animal **documentaries**. His workers were like a talented band, and he was the band's fearless **conductor**.

Knowing he needed more animators, Walt began a school right at the studio! His next project was Disneyland, which he opened in 1955 in Anaheim, California. Presidents and kings visited. Half the people in the country watched its opening day on TV!

"People often ask me if I know the secret of success and if I could tell others how to make their dreams come true. My answer is, you do it by working."

- Walt Disney

19

So Many Accomplishments

During 43 years in Hollywood, Walt produced 68 movies and many TV shows. He still holds the record for the most **Oscars**. Walt Disney founded one of the most famous, successful companies ever by working hard and not giving up!

Stamps from Around the World Honoring Disney's Work

Europe

Africa

North America

Asia

GLOSSARY

animate: to make something, such as a drawing, appear to move by creating a series of drawings and showing them quickly one after another

award: a prize given for doing something

commercial: a break during a TV or radio show that tries to sell something

conductor: a person who stands in front of and directs people as they perform music

documentary: a movie or TV show that tells the facts about real people, events, or things

Great Depression: a period in history when many people were out of work, hungry, or homeless

institute: a company created for a purpose, like learning or helping people

Oscar: a yearly award for the best actors and moviemakers in American film

setback: a problem that makes progress harder and success less likely

FOR MORE INFORMATION

BOOKS

Haldy, Emma E. *Walt Disney*. Ann Arbor, MI: Cherry Lake Publishing, 2017.

Norwich, Grace. *I Am Walt Disney*. New York, NY: Scholastic Inc., 2014.

Tieck, Sarah. *Walt Disney*. Edina, MN: ABDO Publishing Co., 2010.

WEBSITES

American Experience: Walt Disney
pbs.org/wgbh/americanexperience/films/walt-disney/
Watch this awesome movie all about Walt!

The Walt Disney Family Museum
waltdisney.org/walt-disney
This museum in San Francisco, California, is all about Walt Disney!

INDEX